WRITE THE NEXT CHAPTER

Bucket List

THIS BUCKET LIST IS THE CREATION OF

IF FOUND, PLEASE CONTACT ME:

☎

✉

THE MASTER LIST

PAGE	ACTIVITY	DONE		PAGE	ACTIVITY	DONE
2				27		
3				28		
4				29		
5				30		
6				31		
7				32		
8				33		
9				34		
10				35		
11				36		
12				37		
13				38		
14				39		
15				40		
16				41		
17				42		
18				43		
19				44		
20				45		
21				46		
22				47		
23				48		
24				49		
25				50		
26				51		

THE MASTER LIST

PAGE	ACTIVITY	DONE	PAGE	ACTIVITY	DONE
52			77		
53			78		
54			79		
55			80		
56			81		
57			82		
58			83		
59			84		
60			85		
61			86		
62			87		
63			88		
64			89		
65			90		
66			91		
67			92		
68			93		
69			94		
70			95		
71			96		
72			97		
73			98		
74			99		
75			100		
76			101		

IDEA TRIGGERS

ACCOLADE	CREATE	FASCINATING	HOP	MASS	PRECIOUS	REUNIFY	START BALL
ACCOMPLISH	CROWD	FASHION	HOT	MATCH	PREPARED	REUNITE	ROLLING
ACCUMULATE	CRUISING	FATHER	HUDDLE	MATTER	PROBE	REVAMP	START OFF
ACQUIRE	CULTIVATE	FEARLESS	HUMOR	MEET	PROCLAIM	REVEL	STATION
ACT	CURIOUS	FEAST	HUNT	MEET AGAIN	PROCREATE	REVERE	STAY
ACTUALIZE	CUTE	FEAT	IMAGINE	MEMORIALIZE	PRODUCE	REVISE	STEAMY
AD-LIB	DALLIANCE	FEATHER IN CAP	IMPRESS	MEND	PROGRESS	REVITALIZE	STIMULATE
ADVANCE	DAUNTLESS	FESTIVITY	IMPROVE	MERRIMENT	PROJECT	REVIVE	STIR
ADVENTURE	DECISION	FETCHING	IMPROVISE	MERRYMAKING	PROMOTE	RIDE	STOCKPILE
AFFECT CHANGE	DECORATION	FIND	INCIDENT	MILESTONE	PROMPT	RIDING	STOPOVER
AGGREGATE	DEDICATE	FINISH	INCLINED	MIRACLE	PROPEL	RING IN	STORY
ALLURING	DEED	FIRE UP	INCREASE	MOBILIZE	PROSPECT	RISK	STRAIGHTEN OUT
AMASS	DELECTABLE	FIX	INDIVIDUAL	MOOR	PROVIDE	RISQUÉ	STRANGE
AMBROSIAL	DELICIOAUS	FLING	INFLUENCE	MOTIVATE	PROVOCATIVE	ROMANTIC	STRIKE
AMEND	DELIGHT	FLIRTATIOUS	INFORM	MOVE	PROVOKING	ROMP	STRIKING
AMUSEMENT	DELIGHTFUL	FLOCK	INFUSE	MOVEMENT	PUBLICIZE	ROUND UP	SUAVE
ANNIVERSARY	DELIVER	FLYING	INITIATE	MUSTER	PUNCH	ROUSE	SUGGESTIVE
APPEALING	DELVE INTO	FOLLOW	INQUIRING	NAVIGATION	PURIFY	SABBATICAL	SWARM
APPEARANCE	DESIGN	THROUGH	INQUISITIVE	NEGOTIATE	PURSUIT	SAILING	SWING
AROUSE	DESIROUS	FOOLERY	INSPECT	NERVY	PUT	SCARE	TAKE OFF
ASSOCIATE	DEVELOP	FOREIGN	INSPIRIT	OBSERVE	PUZZLED	SCENE	TEASING
ATHLETICS	DEVISE	FORGE	INSTALL	OBTAIN	QUESTIONING	SCHEME	TEST
ATTAIN	DIFFERENT	FORM	INSTILL	OCCASION	QUICKEN	SCHOLARSHIP	THING
AVANT GARDE	DIG INTO	FORMULATE	INSTITUTE	OCCUPATION	QUIET	SCOPE	THRONG
BETTER	DISCOVER	FRAME	INTERESTED	OCCURRENCE	RACK UP	SCORE	THROW DICE
BIKING	DISCOVERY	FREEDOM	INTREPID	OFF-THE-CUFF	RACY	SCOUT	TIME OFF
BIZARRE	DISHY	FRISK	INTRODUCED	ONE AND ONLY	RAFFLE	SEAFARING	TITILLATING
BLESS	DISPORT	FROLIC	INVENT	OPPORTUNITY	RAISE	SEAL	TOUCH
BOLD	DISPOSED	FULFILL	INVEST	ORDER	RAISE HELL	SEARCH	TOUCH UP
BOOST	DISTINCTION	FUN	INVIGORATE	ORGANIZE	RALLY	SECURE	TOUR
BREAKTHROUGH	DISTRACTION	GAIN	INVITE	ORIGINATE	RAMBLE	SEDUCTIVE	TRANSIT
BRING ABOUT	DIVERSION	GAIN GROUND	JEST	OUTLANDISH	RARE	SEEK	TRAVEL
BUILD	DO	GALLANT	JOIN	OUTSIDE CHANCE	REACH	SENSUAL	TRAVERSE
BURROW	DONATION	GALVANIZE	JOKE	OVERHAUL	REACTIVATE	SET DOWN	TREKKING
BUSINESS	DREAM UP	GAME	JOKING	OVERNIGHT	READY	SET IN MOTION	TRIP
CALL UP	DREAMY	GAMING	JUBILATE	PAINT TOWN RED	REALIZE	SET RIGHT	TRIUMPH
CAPER	DRINK TO	GENERATE	JUNKET	PARENT	REASSEMBLE	SET UP	TROPHY
CAPTIVATING	DRIVE	GET	KEEP	PARTY	REASSURE	SETTLE	TRY
CAPTURE	EAGER	GET DONE	KICK UP HEELS	PASS	RECESS	SEXY	TURN ON
CAROUSE	EARN WINGS	GET TOGETHER	KINKY	PASSAGE	RECONCILE	SHAPE UP	TURNING POINT
CAUSE	EFFECT	GIFT	KISSABLE	PASTIME	RECONDITION	SHARPEN	UNAFRAID
CELEBRATION	ELATE	GIVE LIFE TO	LAND	PATCH UP	RECONVENE	SHIFT	UNCOMMON
CEREMONY	ELEVATE	GIVE RISE TO	LANDMARK	PAUSE	RECOVER	SHOT IN THE DARK	UNDERTAKING
CHANCE	EMBOLDEN	GLAMOROUS	LARK	PECULIAR	RECREATE	SIGHTSEEING	UNFAMILIAR
CHARMING	ENACT	GLOBE-TROTTING	LAUD	PEREGRINE	RECREATION	SIGN	UNFLINCHING
CHOOSE	ENDOWMENT	GLORIFY	LAY FOUNDATION	PERFECT	RECTIFY	SIRE	UNITE
CIRCUMSTANCE	ENERGIZE	GO INTO	LEAP	PERFORM	RECUPERATE	SITUATION	UNUSUAL
CLEANSE	ENHANCE	GOLD STAR	LET LOOSE	PERK UP	REFINE	SKYROCKET	UP FOR
CLUSTER	ENKINDLE	GRANT	LIBIDINOUS	PERSEVERING	REFORM	SOJOURN	UPGRADE
COINCIDENCE	ENLIVEN	GROUND	LINE	PERSISTENT	REFRESH	SOLVE	VACATION
COLLECT	ENTERPRISE	GROUP	LIVE	PHASE	REFURBISH	SPARE MOMENTS	VALIANT
COLORFUL	ENTICING	HALLOW	LIVE IT UP	PHENOMENON	REJOICE	SPARE TIME	VALOROUS
COME UP WITH	ENVISION	HANG AROUND	LODGE	PICK UP	REJOIN	SPARK	VENTURE
COME-HITHER	ESTABLISH	HANG OUT	LONG SHOT	PILE UP	REKINDLE	SPAWN	VOYAGE
COMPLETE	EVENING	HAPPENING	LOOK INTO	PLACE	RELAXATION	SPEC	WAGER
COMPOSE	EVENT	HAPPINESS	LOOK UP	PLAN	REMAKE	SPECULATION	WALK
CONCEIVE	EXALT	HARDY	LOTTERY	PLAY	REMODEL	SPICY	WANDER
CONCENTRATE	EXAMINE	HATCH	LUSCIOUS	PLEASING	RENEW	SPIRITED	WANDERLUST
CONCLUDE	EXCITE	HAVE A BALL	MAKE	PLEASURE	REPAIR	SPORT	WAY OUT
CONCOCT	EXCLUSIVE	HAVE A LOOK	MAKE MERRY	PLUCK	RESEARCH	SPORTS	WAYFARING
CONGREGATE	EXCURSION	HEAP	MAKE OVER	PLUCKY	RESOLUTE	SPRUCE	WEEKEND
CONSECRATE	EXHILARATE	HEARTEN	MAKE STRIDES	POKE	RESOLVE	SPRUCE UP	WEIRD
CONSTRUCT	EXPEDITION	HEAVENLY	MAKE THE SCENE	POLISH	REST	SPUNKY	WIN
CONTINGENCY	EXPERIENCE	HELP	MAKE UP	POUR IN	RESTORE	SPUR	WING
CONVERGE	EXTERNAL	HEROIC	MAKE WHOOPEE	PRACTICE	RESURRECT	STABILIZE	WONDER
COOK UP	EXTRAORDINARY	HOLIDAY	MANAGE	PRAISE	RETIREMENT	STACK UP	WORK UP
COURAGEOUS	FAR OUT	HONOR	MARVEL	PRANK	RETRIEVE	START	WRITE

PRIORITY ☆☆☆☆☆

ITEM #1: _____

I WANT TO DO THIS BECAUSE...

_____

_____

_____

MAKE IT HAPPEN: HOW? WHEN?

_____

_____

_____

_____

REVIEW

DATE COMPLETED: / /

WHAT HAPPENED? (PEOPLE MET, HIGH POINTS, CHALLENGES, EXPECTATIONS VS REALITY)

_____

_____

_____

_____

THE **BEST PART** WAS...

_____

_____

_____

_____

_____

BUDGET

$

ANTICIPATED DATE

/ /   TO   / /

ACTION LIST

⊘
⊘
⊘
⊘
⊘
⊘
⊘
⊘
⊘

SUCCESS!

✓

PLACE A CHECK HERE TO
TAKE IT OFF YOUR BUCKET LIST

RATE THIS ACTIVITY

☆☆☆☆☆

I WANT TO DO THIS BECAUSE...

_____
_____
_____
_____

MAKE IT HAPPEN: HOW? WHEN?

_____
_____
_____
_____

REVIEW

DATE COMPLETED: /   /

WHAT HAPPENED? (PEOPLE MET, HIGH POINTS, CHALLENGES, EXPECTATIONS VS REALITY)

_____
_____
_____
_____

THE **BEST PART** WAS...

_____
_____
_____
_____
_____

BUDGET

$

ANTICIPATED DATE

/ /   TO   / /

ACTION LIST

⊘
⊘
⊘
⊘
⊘
⊘
⊘
⊘
⊘

SUCCESS! ✓

PLACE A CHECK HERE TO
TAKE IT OFF YOUR BUCKET LIST

RATE THIS ACTIVITY

☆☆☆☆☆

I WANT TO DO THIS BECAUSE...

_____

_____

_____

_____

MAKE IT HAPPEN: HOW? WHEN?

_____

_____

_____

_____

REVIEW

DATE COMPLETED: / /

_____

WHAT HAPPENED? (PEOPLE MET, HIGH POINTS, CHALLENGES, EXPECTATIONS VS REALITY)

_____

_____

_____

_____

THE **BEST PART** WAS...

_____

_____

_____

_____

_____

BUDGET

$

ANTICIPATED DATE

/ /   TO   / /

ACTION LIST

⊘ _____
⊘ _____
⊘ _____
⊘ _____
⊘ _____
⊘ _____
⊘ _____
⊘ _____
⊘ _____
⊘ _____

SUCCESS! ✓

PLACE A CHECK HERE TO
TAKE IT OFF YOUR BUCKET LIST

RATE THIS ACTIVITY

☆☆☆☆☆

I WANT TO DO THIS BECAUSE...

_____

_____

_____

_____

MAKE IT HAPPEN: HOW? WHEN?

_____

_____

_____

_____

REVIEW

DATE COMPLETED: / /

WHAT HAPPENED? (PEOPLE MET, HIGH POINTS, CHALLENGES, EXPECTATIONS VS REALITY)

_____

_____

_____

_____

THE **BEST PART** WAS...

_____

_____

_____

_____

_____

BUDGET

$

ANTICIPATED DATE

/ /   TO   / /

ACTION LIST

⊘
⊘
⊘
⊘
⊘
⊘
⊘
⊘

SUCCESS! ✓

PLACE A CHECK HERE TO
TAKE IT OFF YOUR BUCKET LIST

RATE THIS ACTIVITY

☆☆☆☆☆

REST IS NOT IDLENESS, AND TO LIE SOMETIMES ON THE GRASS UNDER TREES ON A SUMMER'S DAY, LISTENING TO THE MURMUR
OF THE WATER, OR WATCHING THE CLOUDS FLOAT ACROSS THE SKY, IS BY NO MEANS A WASTE OF TIME. LUBBOCK

I WANT TO DO THIS BECAUSE...

MAKE IT HAPPEN: HOW? WHEN?

REVIEW

DATE COMPLETED: / /

WHAT HAPPENED? (PEOPLE MET, HIGH POINTS, CHALLENGES, EXPECTATIONS VS REALITY)

THE **BEST PART** WAS...

BUDGET

$

ANTICIPATED DATE

/ /   TO   / /

ACTION LIST

- ⊘
- ⊘
- ⊘
- ⊘
- ⊘
- ⊘
- ⊘
- ⊘
- ⊘

SUCCESS! ✓

PLACE A CHECK HERE TO
TAKE IT OFF YOUR BUCKET LIST

RATE THIS ACTIVITY

☆☆☆☆☆

I WANT TO DO THIS BECAUSE...

_____

_____

_____

_____

MAKE IT HAPPEN: HOW? WHEN?

_____

_____

_____

_____

REVIEW

DATE COMPLETED: /   /

WHAT HAPPENED? (PEOPLE MET, HIGH POINTS, CHALLENGES, EXPECTATIONS VS REALITY)

_____

_____

_____

_____

THE **BEST PART** WAS...

_____

_____

_____

_____

_____

BUDGET

$

ANTICIPATED DATE

/ /   TO   / /

ACTION LIST

⊘
⊘
⊘
⊘
⊘
⊘
⊘
⊘
⊘

SUCCESS!

✓

PLACE A CHECK HERE TO
TAKE IT OFF YOUR BUCKET LIST

RATE THIS ACTIVITY

☆☆☆☆☆

PRIORITY ☆☆☆☆☆　　　ITEM #7: _____

I WANT TO DO THIS BECAUSE...

_____

_____

_____

_____

MAKE IT HAPPEN: HOW? WHEN?

_____

_____

_____

_____

REVIEW

DATE COMPLETED:　　/　/

WHAT HAPPENED? (PEOPLE MET, HIGH POINTS, CHALLENGES, EXPECTATIONS VS REALITY)

_____

_____

_____

_____

THE **BEST PART** WAS...

_____

_____

_____

_____

_____

BUDGET

$

ANTICIPATED DATE

/　/　　TO　　/　/

ACTION LIST

- ⊘
- ⊘
- ⊘
- ⊘
- ⊘
- ⊘
- ⊘
- ⊘
- ⊘

SUCCESS! ✓

PLACE A CHECK HERE TO
TAKE IT OFF YOUR BUCKET LIST

RATE THIS ACTIVITY

☆☆☆☆☆

I WANT TO DO THIS BECAUSE...

_____

_____

_____

MAKE IT HAPPEN: HOW? WHEN?

_____

_____

_____

_____

REVIEW

DATE COMPLETED: /   /

WHAT HAPPENED? (PEOPLE MET, HIGH POINTS, CHALLENGES, EXPECTATIONS VS REALITY)

_____

_____

_____

_____

THE **BEST PART** WAS...

_____

_____

_____

_____

_____

BUDGET

$

ANTICIPATED DATE

/   /   TO   /   /

ACTION LIST

⊘
⊘
⊘
⊘
⊘
⊘
⊘
⊘
⊘

SUCCESS! ✓

PLACE A CHECK HERE TO
TAKE IT OFF YOUR BUCKET LIST

RATE THIS ACTIVITY

☆☆☆☆☆

PRIORITY ☆☆☆☆☆   ITEM #9: _____

I WANT TO DO THIS BECAUSE...

_____

_____

_____

_____

MAKE IT HAPPEN: HOW? WHEN?

_____

_____

_____

_____

REVIEW

DATE COMPLETED: /   /

_____

WHAT HAPPENED? (PEOPLE MET, HIGH POINTS, CHALLENGES, EXPECTATIONS VS REALITY)

_____

_____

_____

_____

_____

THE **BEST PART** WAS...

_____

_____

_____

_____

_____

BUDGET
$

ANTICIPATED DATE
/ /   TO   / /

ACTION LIST

⊘ _____
⊘ _____
⊘ _____
⊘ _____
⊘ _____
⊘ _____
⊘ _____
⊘ _____
⊘ _____

SUCCESS!

PLACE A CHECK HERE TO
TAKE IT OFF YOUR BUCKET LIST

RATE THIS ACTIVITY

☆☆☆☆☆

I WANT TO DO THIS BECAUSE...

_____

_____

_____

_____

MAKE IT HAPPEN: HOW? WHEN?

_____

_____

_____

_____

REVIEW

DATE COMPLETED: /   /

WHAT HAPPENED? (PEOPLE MET, HIGH POINTS, CHALLENGES, EXPECTATIONS VS REALITY)

_____

_____

_____

_____

_____

THE **BEST PART** WAS...

_____

_____

_____

_____

_____

BUDGET

$

ANTICIPATED DATE

/ /   TO   / /

ACTION LIST

⊘
⊘
⊘
⊘
⊘
⊘
⊘
⊘
⊘

SUCCESS! ✓

PLACE A CHECK HERE TO
TAKE IT OFF YOUR BUCKET LIST

RATE THIS ACTIVITY

☆☆☆☆☆

I WANT TO DO THIS BECAUSE...

_____

_____

_____

_____

MAKE IT HAPPEN: HOW? WHEN?

_____

_____

_____

_____

REVIEW

DATE COMPLETED: / /

WHAT HAPPENED? (PEOPLE MET, HIGH POINTS, CHALLENGES, EXPECTATIONS VS REALITY)

_____

_____

_____

_____

_____

THE **BEST PART** WAS...

_____

_____

_____

_____

_____

BUDGET

$ _____

ANTICIPATED DATE

/ /   TO   / /

ACTION LIST

- ⊘
- ⊘
- ⊘
- ⊘
- ⊘
- ⊘
- ⊘
- ⊘
- ⊘

SUCCESS! ✓

PLACE A CHECK HERE TO
TAKE IT OFF YOUR BUCKET LIST

RATE THIS ACTIVITY

☆☆☆☆☆

I WANT TO DO THIS BECAUSE...

MAKE IT HAPPEN: HOW? WHEN?

REVIEW

DATE COMPLETED: / /

WHAT HAPPENED? (PEOPLE MET, HIGH POINTS, CHALLENGES, EXPECTATIONS VS REALITY)

THE **BEST PART** WAS...

BUDGET

$

ANTICIPATED DATE

/ /   TO   / /

ACTION LIST

- ⊘
- ⊘
- ⊘
- ⊘
- ⊘
- ⊘
- ⊘
- ⊘
- ⊘

SUCCESS!

PLACE A CHECK HERE TO
TAKE IT OFF YOUR BUCKET LIST

RATE THIS ACTIVITY

☆☆☆☆☆

I WANT TO DO THIS BECAUSE...

_____

_____

_____

MAKE IT HAPPEN: HOW? WHEN?

_____

_____

_____

_____

REVIEW

DATE COMPLETED: / /

WHAT HAPPENED? (PEOPLE MET, HIGH POINTS, CHALLENGES, EXPECTATIONS VS REALITY)

_____

_____

_____

_____

_____

THE **BEST PART** WAS...

_____

_____

_____

_____

_____

BUDGET

$

ANTICIPATED DATE

/ /   TO   / /

ACTION LIST

⊘
⊘
⊘
⊘
⊘
⊘
⊘
⊘
⊘

SUCCESS!

PLACE A CHECK HERE TO
TAKE IT OFF YOUR BUCKET LIST

RATE THIS ACTIVITY

☆☆☆☆☆

I WANT TO DO THIS BECAUSE...

_____

_____

_____

_____

MAKE IT HAPPEN: HOW? WHEN?

_____

_____

_____

_____

_____

REVIEW

DATE COMPLETED: / /

WHAT HAPPENED? (PEOPLE MET, HIGH POINTS, CHALLENGES, EXPECTATIONS VS REALITY)

_____

_____

_____

_____

_____

THE **BEST PART** WAS...

_____

_____

_____

_____

_____

BUDGET

$

ANTICIPATED DATE

/ /   TO   / /

ACTION LIST

⊘
⊘
⊘
⊘
⊘
⊘
⊘
⊘
⊘

SUCCESS! ✓

PLACE A CHECK HERE TO
TAKE IT OFF YOUR BUCKET LIST

RATE THIS ACTIVITY

☆☆☆☆☆

I WANT TO DO THIS BECAUSE...

_____
_____
_____
_____

MAKE IT HAPPEN: HOW? WHEN?

_____
_____
_____
_____

REVIEW

DATE COMPLETED: / /

_____

WHAT HAPPENED? (PEOPLE MET, HIGH POINTS, CHALLENGES, EXPECTATIONS VS REALITY)

_____
_____
_____
_____
_____

THE **BEST PART** WAS...

_____
_____
_____
_____
_____
_____

BUDGET

$

ANTICIPATED DATE

/ /   TO   / /

ACTION LIST

- ⊘
- ⊘
- ⊘
- ⊘
- ⊘
- ⊘
- ⊘
- ⊘
- ⊘
- ⊘

SUCCESS! ✓

PLACE A CHECK HERE TO
TAKE IT OFF YOUR BUCKET LIST

RATE THIS ACTIVITY

☆☆☆☆☆

ANOTHER GOOD THING ABOUT BEING POOR IS THAT WHEN YOU ARE SEVENTY YOUR CHILDREN WILL NOT HAVE
DECLARED YOU LEGALLY INSANE IN ORDER TO GAIN CONTROL OF YOUR ESTATE. WOODY ALLEN

I WANT TO DO THIS BECAUSE...

_____

_____

_____

_____

MAKE IT HAPPEN: HOW? WHEN?

_____

_____

_____

_____

REVIEW

DATE COMPLETED: / /

WHAT HAPPENED? (PEOPLE MET, HIGH POINTS, CHALLENGES, EXPECTATIONS VS REALITY)

_____

_____

_____

_____

THE **BEST PART** WAS...

_____

_____

_____

_____

_____

BUDGET

$

ANTICIPATED DATE

/ /   TO   / /

ACTION LIST

⊘
⊘
⊘
⊘
⊘
⊘
⊘
⊘
⊘

SUCCESS! ✓

PLACE A CHECK HERE TO
TAKE IT OFF YOUR BUCKET LIST

RATE THIS ACTIVITY

☆☆☆☆☆

I ADVISE YOU TO GO ON LIVING SOLELY TO ENRAGE THOSE WHO ARE PAYING YOUR ANNUITIES; IT IS THE ONLY PLEASURE I HAVE LEFT. VOLTAIRE

I WANT TO DO THIS BECAUSE...

_____

_____

_____

MAKE IT HAPPEN: HOW? WHEN?

_____

_____

_____

_____

REVIEW

DATE COMPLETED: / /

WHAT HAPPENED? (PEOPLE MET, HIGH POINTS, CHALLENGES, EXPECTATIONS VS REALITY)

_____

_____

_____

_____

THE **BEST PART** WAS...

_____

_____

_____

_____

_____

BUDGET

$

ANTICIPATED DATE

/ /   TO   / /

ACTION LIST

- ⊘
- ⊘
- ⊘
- ⊘
- ⊘
- ⊘
- ⊘
- ⊘
- ⊘

SUCCESS! ✓

PLACE A CHECK HERE TO TAKE IT OFF YOUR BUCKET LIST

RATE THIS ACTIVITY

☆☆☆☆☆

I WANT TO DO THIS BECAUSE...

MAKE IT HAPPEN: HOW? WHEN?

REVIEW

DATE COMPLETED: / /

WHAT HAPPENED? (PEOPLE MET, HIGH POINTS, CHALLENGES, EXPECTATIONS VS REALITY)

THE **BEST PART** WAS...

BUDGET

$

ANTICIPATED DATE

/ /   TO   / /

ACTION LIST

⊘
⊘
⊘
⊘
⊘
⊘
⊘
⊘
⊘

SUCCESS!

PLACE A CHECK HERE TO
TAKE IT OFF YOUR BUCKET LIST

RATE THIS ACTIVITY

☆☆☆☆☆

I WANT TO DO THIS BECAUSE...

_____
_____
_____
_____

MAKE IT HAPPEN: HOW? WHEN?

_____
_____
_____
_____
_____

REVIEW

DATE COMPLETED: / /

WHAT HAPPENED? (PEOPLE MET, HIGH POINTS, CHALLENGES, EXPECTATIONS VS REALITY)

_____
_____
_____
_____
_____

THE **BEST PART** WAS...

_____
_____
_____
_____
_____
_____

BUDGET

$

ANTICIPATED DATE

/ /   TO   / /

ACTION LIST

- ⊘
- ⊘
- ⊘
- ⊘
- ⊘
- ⊘
- ⊘
- ⊘
- ⊘

SUCCESS! ✓

PLACE A CHECK HERE TO
TAKE IT OFF YOUR BUCKET LIST

RATE THIS ACTIVITY

☆☆☆☆☆

ITEM #20: _____

I WANT TO DO THIS BECAUSE...

_____

_____

_____

MAKE IT HAPPEN: HOW? WHEN?

_____

_____

_____

_____

REVIEW

DATE COMPLETED: / /

WHAT HAPPENED? (PEOPLE MET, HIGH POINTS, CHALLENGES, EXPECTATIONS VS REALITY)

_____

_____

_____

_____

THE **BEST PART** WAS...

_____

_____

_____

_____

_____

BUDGET

$

ANTICIPATED DATE

/ /   TO   / /

ACTION LIST

⊘
⊘
⊘
⊘
⊘
⊘
⊘
⊘
⊘

SUCCESS!

✓

PLACE A CHECK HERE TO
TAKE IT OFF YOUR BUCKET LIST

RATE THIS ACTIVITY

☆☆☆☆☆

I WANT TO DO THIS BECAUSE...

BUDGET

$

ANTICIPATED DATE

/ /   TO   / /

MAKE IT HAPPEN: HOW? WHEN?

ACTION LIST

REVIEW

DATE COMPLETED: / /

WHAT HAPPENED? (PEOPLE MET, HIGH POINTS, CHALLENGES, EXPECTATIONS VS REALITY)

SUCCESS!

PLACE A CHECK HERE TO
TAKE IT OFF YOUR BUCKET LIST

THE **BEST PART** WAS...

RATE THIS ACTIVITY

☆☆☆☆☆

I WANT TO DO THIS BECAUSE...

_____

_____

_____

_____

MAKE IT HAPPEN: HOW? WHEN?

_____

_____

_____

_____

REVIEW

DATE COMPLETED: / /

WHAT HAPPENED? (PEOPLE MET, HIGH POINTS, CHALLENGES, EXPECTATIONS VS REALITY)

_____

_____

_____

_____

THE **BEST PART** WAS...

_____

_____

_____

_____

_____

BUDGET

$

ANTICIPATED DATE

/ /   TO   / /

ACTION LIST

⊘
⊘
⊘
⊘
⊘
⊘
⊘
⊘
⊘
⊘

SUCCESS!

✓

PLACE A CHECK HERE TO
TAKE IT OFF YOUR BUCKET LIST

RATE THIS ACTIVITY

☆☆☆☆☆

PRIORITY ☆☆☆☆☆   ITEM #23: _____

I WANT TO DO THIS BECAUSE...

_____
_____
_____
_____

MAKE IT HAPPEN: HOW? WHEN?

_____
_____
_____
_____

REVIEW

DATE COMPLETED: / /

WHAT HAPPENED? (PEOPLE MET, HIGH POINTS, CHALLENGES,
EXPECTATIONS VS REALITY)

_____
_____
_____
_____
_____

THE **BEST PART** WAS...

_____
_____
_____
_____
_____

BUDGET

$

ANTICIPATED DATE

/ /   TO   / /

ACTION LIST

⊘ _____
⊘ _____
⊘ _____
⊘ _____
⊘ _____
⊘ _____
⊘ _____
⊘ _____
⊘ _____

SUCCESS!
✓

PLACE A CHECK HERE TO
TAKE IT OFF YOUR BUCKET LIST

RATE THIS ACTIVITY

☆☆☆☆☆

I WANT TO DO THIS BECAUSE...

_____

_____

_____

_____

MAKE IT HAPPEN: HOW? WHEN?

_____

_____

_____

_____

REVIEW

DATE COMPLETED: / /

WHAT HAPPENED? (PEOPLE MET, HIGH POINTS, CHALLENGES, EXPECTATIONS VS REALITY)

_____

_____

_____

_____

THE **BEST PART** WAS...

_____

_____

_____

_____

BUDGET

$

ANTICIPATED DATE

/ /   TO   / /

ACTION LIST

⊘
⊘
⊘
⊘
⊘
⊘
⊘
⊘
⊘

SUCCESS! ✓

PLACE A CHECK HERE TO
TAKE IT OFF YOUR BUCKET LIST

RATE THIS ACTIVITY

☆☆☆☆☆

WHEN A MAN RETIRES AND TIME IS NO LONGER A MATTER OF URGENT IMPORTANCE, HIS
COLLEAGUES GENERALLY PRESENT HIM WITH A WATCH. R. C. SHERRIFF

PRIORITY ☆☆☆☆☆   ITEM #25: _____

I WANT TO DO THIS BECAUSE...	**BUDGET**
	$
	ANTICIPATED DATE
	/ / TO / /
MAKE IT HAPPEN: HOW? WHEN?	**ACTION LIST**

REVIEW

DATE COMPLETED: / /

WHAT HAPPENED? (PEOPLE MET, HIGH POINTS, CHALLENGES, EXPECTATIONS VS REALITY)

SUCCESS!

PLACE A CHECK HERE TO
TAKE IT OFF YOUR BUCKET LIST

THE **BEST PART** WAS...

RATE THIS ACTIVITY

☆☆☆☆☆

I WANT TO DO THIS BECAUSE...

_____

_____

_____

_____

MAKE IT HAPPEN: HOW? WHEN?

_____

_____

_____

_____

REVIEW

DATE COMPLETED: ___ / ___ / ___

_____

WHAT HAPPENED? (PEOPLE MET, HIGH POINTS, CHALLENGES, EXPECTATIONS VS REALITY)

_____

_____

_____

_____

THE **BEST PART** WAS...

_____

_____

_____

_____

BUDGET

$

ANTICIPATED DATE

/ /   TO   / /

ACTION LIST

⊘
⊘
⊘
⊘
⊘
⊘
⊘
⊘
⊘

SUCCESS! ✓

PLACE A CHECK HERE TO
TAKE IT OFF YOUR BUCKET LIST

RATE THIS ACTIVITY

☆☆☆☆☆

PRIORITY ☆☆☆☆☆   ITEM #27: _____

I WANT TO DO THIS BECAUSE...

_____

_____

_____

_____

MAKE IT HAPPEN: HOW? WHEN?

_____

_____

_____

_____

REVIEW

DATE COMPLETED: / /

WHAT HAPPENED? (PEOPLE MET, HIGH POINTS, CHALLENGES, EXPECTATIONS VS REALITY)

_____

_____

_____

_____

_____

THE **BEST PART** WAS...

_____

_____

_____

_____

_____

BUDGET

$

ANTICIPATED DATE

/ /   TO   / /

ACTION LIST

- ⊘ _____
- ⊘ _____
- ⊘ _____
- ⊘ _____
- ⊘ _____
- ⊘ _____
- ⊘ _____
- ⊘ _____
- ⊘ _____

SUCCESS!

✓

PLACE A CHECK HERE TO
TAKE IT OFF YOUR BUCKET LIST

RATE THIS ACTIVITY

☆☆☆☆☆

SOMETHING PRETTY... THAT'S JUST THE SURFACE; PEOPLE WORRY SO MUCH ABOUT AGING, BUT YOU LOOK YOUNGER IF YOU DON'T WORRY ABOUT IT. JEANNE MOREAU

27

I WANT TO DO THIS BECAUSE...

_____
_____
_____
_____

MAKE IT HAPPEN: HOW? WHEN?

_____
_____
_____
_____

REVIEW

DATE COMPLETED: /   /

WHAT HAPPENED? (PEOPLE MET, HIGH POINTS, CHALLENGES, EXPECTATIONS VS REALITY)

_____
_____
_____
_____

THE **BEST PART** WAS...

_____
_____
_____
_____

BUDGET

$

ANTICIPATED DATE

/ /   TO   / /

ACTION LIST

- ⊘
- ⊘
- ⊘
- ⊘
- ⊘
- ⊘
- ⊘
- ⊘
- ⊘

SUCCESS!

✓

PLACE A CHECK HERE TO
TAKE IT OFF YOUR BUCKET LIST

RATE THIS ACTIVITY

☆☆☆☆☆

IT'S PARADOXICAL THAT THE IDEA OF LIVING A LONG LIFE APPEALS TO EVERYONE, BUT THE
IDEA OF GETTING OLD DOESN'T APPEAL TO ANYONE. ANDY ROONEY

PRIORITY ☆☆☆☆☆

I WANT TO DO THIS BECAUSE...

BUDGET

$

ANTICIPATED DATE

/ /   TO   / /

MAKE IT HAPPEN: HOW? WHEN?

ACTION LIST

⊘
⊘
⊘
⊘
⊘
⊘
⊘
⊘
⊘

REVIEW

DATE COMPLETED: / /

WHAT HAPPENED? (PEOPLE MET, HIGH POINTS, CHALLENGES, EXPECTATIONS VS REALITY)

SUCCESS!

✓

PLACE A CHECK HERE TO
TAKE IT OFF YOUR BUCKET LIST

THE **BEST PART** WAS...

RATE THIS ACTIVITY

☆☆☆☆☆

I WANT TO DO THIS BECAUSE...

_____

_____

_____

_____

MAKE IT HAPPEN: HOW? WHEN?

_____

_____

_____

_____

REVIEW

DATE COMPLETED: / /

_____

WHAT HAPPENED? (PEOPLE MET, HIGH POINTS, CHALLENGES, EXPECTATIONS VS REALITY)

_____

_____

_____

_____

THE **BEST PART** WAS...

_____

_____

_____

_____

_____

BUDGET

$

ANTICIPATED DATE

/ /   TO   / /

ACTION LIST

⊘ _____
⊘ _____
⊘ _____
⊘ _____
⊘ _____
⊘ _____
⊘ _____
⊘ _____
⊘ _____

SUCCESS! ✓

PLACE A CHECK HERE TO
TAKE IT OFF YOUR BUCKET LIST

RATE THIS ACTIVITY

☆☆☆☆☆

I WANT TO DO THIS BECAUSE...

_____

_____

_____

MAKE IT HAPPEN: HOW? WHEN?

_____

_____

_____

_____

REVIEW

DATE COMPLETED: / /

_____

WHAT HAPPENED? (PEOPLE MET, HIGH POINTS, CHALLENGES, EXPECTATIONS VS REALITY)

_____

_____

_____

_____

THE **BEST PART** WAS...

_____

_____

_____

_____

_____

BUDGET

$

ANTICIPATED DATE

/ /   TO   / /

ACTION LIST

- ⊘
- ⊘
- ⊘
- ⊘
- ⊘
- ⊘
- ⊘
- ⊘
- ⊘

SUCCESS!

✓

PLACE A CHECK HERE TO
TAKE IT OFF YOUR BUCKET LIST

RATE THIS ACTIVITY

☆☆☆☆☆

RETIREMENT MAY BE LOOKED UPON EITHER AS A PROLONGED HOLIDAY OR AS A REJECTION, A BEING THROWN ON TO THE SCRAP-HEAP. SIMONE DE BEAUVOIR

(31)

I WANT TO DO THIS BECAUSE...

MAKE IT HAPPEN: HOW? WHEN?

REVIEW

DATE COMPLETED: / /

WHAT HAPPENED? (PEOPLE MET, HIGH POINTS, CHALLENGES, EXPECTATIONS VS REALITY)

THE **BEST PART** WAS...

BUDGET

$

ANTICIPATED DATE

/ /   TO   / /

ACTION LIST

⊘
⊘
⊘
⊘
⊘
⊘
⊘
⊘
⊘

SUCCESS! ✓

PLACE A CHECK HERE TO
TAKE IT OFF YOUR BUCKET LIST

RATE THIS ACTIVITY

☆☆☆☆☆

A RETIRED HUSBAND IS OFTEN A WIFE'S FULL-TIME JOB. ELLA HARRIS

I WANT TO DO THIS BECAUSE...

_____
_____
_____
_____

MAKE IT HAPPEN: HOW? WHEN?

_____
_____
_____
_____

REVIEW

DATE COMPLETED: / /

_____

WHAT HAPPENED? (PEOPLE MET, HIGH POINTS, CHALLENGES, EXPECTATIONS VS REALITY)

_____
_____
_____
_____

THE **BEST PART** WAS...

_____
_____
_____
_____
_____

BUDGET

$

ANTICIPATED DATE

/ /   TO   / /

ACTION LIST

○ _____
○ _____
○ _____
○ _____
○ _____
○ _____
○ _____
○ _____
○ _____
○ _____

SUCCESS! ✓

PLACE A CHECK HERE TO
TAKE IT OFF YOUR BUCKET LIST

RATE THIS ACTIVITY

☆☆☆☆☆

I WANT TO DO THIS BECAUSE...

_____

_____

_____

MAKE IT HAPPEN: HOW? WHEN?

_____

_____

_____

_____

REVIEW

DATE COMPLETED:　　/ /

_____

WHAT HAPPENED? (PEOPLE MET, HIGH POINTS, CHALLENGES, EXPECTATIONS VS REALITY)

_____

_____

_____

_____

THE **BEST PART** WAS...

_____

_____

_____

_____

_____

BUDGET

$

ANTICIPATED DATE

/ /　　TO　　/ /

ACTION LIST

⊘ _____
⊘ _____
⊘ _____
⊘ _____
⊘ _____
⊘ _____
⊘ _____
⊘ _____

SUCCESS! ✓

PLACE A CHECK HERE TO
TAKE IT OFF YOUR BUCKET LIST

RATE THIS ACTIVITY

☆☆☆☆☆

ITEM #35: _____

I WANT TO DO THIS BECAUSE...

_____

_____

_____

_____

MAKE IT HAPPEN: HOW? WHEN?

_____

_____

_____

_____

REVIEW

DATE COMPLETED: / /

WHAT HAPPENED? (PEOPLE MET, HIGH POINTS, CHALLENGES, EXPECTATIONS VS REALITY)

_____

_____

_____

_____

_____

THE **BEST PART** WAS...

_____

_____

_____

_____

_____

_____

BUDGET

$

ANTICIPATED DATE

/ /   TO   / /

ACTION LIST

- ⊘
- ⊘
- ⊘
- ⊘
- ⊘
- ⊘
- ⊘
- ⊘
- ⊘

SUCCESS!

✓

PLACE A CHECK HERE TO
TAKE IT OFF YOUR BUCKET LIST

RATE THIS ACTIVITY

☆☆☆☆☆

I WANT TO DO THIS BECAUSE...

_____

_____

_____

_____

MAKE IT HAPPEN: HOW? WHEN?

_____

_____

_____

_____

REVIEW

DATE COMPLETED: ./ /

WHAT HAPPENED? (PEOPLE MET, HIGH POINTS, CHALLENGES, EXPECTATIONS VS REALITY)

_____

_____

_____

_____

THE **BEST PART** WAS...

_____

_____

_____

_____

_____

BUDGET

$

ANTICIPATED DATE

/ /   TO   / /

ACTION LIST

⊘
⊘
⊘
⊘
⊘
⊘
⊘
⊘
⊘

SUCCESS! ✓

PLACE A CHECK HERE TO
TAKE IT OFF YOUR BUCKET LIST

RATE THIS ACTIVITY

☆☆☆☆☆

PRIORITY ☆☆☆☆☆   ITEM #37: _____

I WANT TO DO THIS BECAUSE...

_____

_____

_____

_____

MAKE IT HAPPEN: HOW? WHEN?

_____

_____

_____

_____

REVIEW

DATE COMPLETED: / /

WHAT HAPPENED? (PEOPLE MET, HIGH POINTS, CHALLENGES, EXPECTATIONS VS REALITY)

_____

_____

_____

_____

THE **BEST PART** WAS...

_____

_____

_____

_____

_____

BUDGET

$

ANTICIPATED DATE

/ /   TO   / /

ACTION LIST

⊘
⊘
⊘
⊘
⊘
⊘
⊘
⊘
⊘

SUCCESS! ✓

PLACE A CHECK HERE TO
TAKE IT OFF YOUR BUCKET LIST

RATE THIS ACTIVITY

☆☆☆☆☆

I WANT TO DO THIS BECAUSE...

_____
_____
_____
_____

MAKE IT HAPPEN: HOW? WHEN?

_____
_____
_____
_____

REVIEW

DATE COMPLETED: / /

WHAT HAPPENED? (PEOPLE MET, HIGH POINTS, CHALLENGES, EXPECTATIONS VS REALITY)

_____
_____
_____
_____

THE **BEST PART** WAS...

_____
_____
_____
_____

BUDGET

$

ANTICIPATED DATE

/ /   TO   / /

ACTION LIST

- ⊘
- ⊘
- ⊘
- ⊘
- ⊘
- ⊘
- ⊘
- ⊘
- ⊘

SUCCESS! ✓

PLACE A CHECK HERE TO
TAKE IT OFF YOUR BUCKET LIST

RATE THIS ACTIVITY

☆☆☆☆☆

ITEM #39: _____

I WANT TO DO THIS BECAUSE...

_____
_____
_____
_____

MAKE IT HAPPEN: HOW? WHEN?

_____
_____
_____
_____

REVIEW

DATE COMPLETED: / /

WHAT HAPPENED? (PEOPLE MET, HIGH POINTS, CHALLENGES, EXPECTATIONS VS REALITY)

_____
_____
_____
_____
_____

THE **BEST PART** WAS...

_____
_____
_____
_____
_____

BUDGET

$

ANTICIPATED DATE

/ /   TO   / /

ACTION LIST

⊘ _____
⊘ _____
⊘ _____
⊘ _____
⊘ _____
⊘ _____
⊘ _____
⊘ _____
⊘ _____

SUCCESS! ✓

PLACE A CHECK HERE TO
TAKE IT OFF YOUR BUCKET LIST

RATE THIS ACTIVITY

☆☆☆☆☆

I WANT TO DO THIS BECAUSE...

_____

_____

_____

_____

MAKE IT HAPPEN: HOW? WHEN?

_____

_____

_____

_____

REVIEW

DATE COMPLETED: /   /

_____

WHAT HAPPENED? (PEOPLE MET, HIGH POINTS, CHALLENGES, EXPECTATIONS VS REALITY)

_____

_____

_____

_____

THE **BEST PART** WAS...

_____

_____

_____

_____

BUDGET

$

ANTICIPATED DATE

/ /   TO   / /

ACTION LIST

- ⊘
- ⊘
- ⊘
- ⊘
- ⊘
- ⊘
- ⊘
- ⊘
- ⊘

SUCCESS! ✓

PLACE A CHECK HERE TO
TAKE IT OFF YOUR BUCKET LIST

RATE THIS ACTIVITY

☆☆☆☆☆

PRIORITY ☆☆☆☆☆   ITEM #41: _____

I WANT TO DO THIS BECAUSE...

_____

_____

_____

_____

MAKE IT HAPPEN: HOW? WHEN?

_____

_____

_____

_____

REVIEW

DATE COMPLETED: / /

WHAT HAPPENED? (PEOPLE MET, HIGH POINTS, CHALLENGES, EXPECTATIONS VS REALITY)

_____

_____

_____

_____

THE **BEST PART** WAS...

_____

_____

_____

_____

_____

BUDGET

$

ANTICIPATED DATE

/ /   TO   / /

ACTION LIST

⊘
⊘
⊘
⊘
⊘
⊘
⊘
⊘
⊘

SUCCESS!

✓

PLACE A CHECK HERE TO
TAKE IT OFF YOUR BUCKET LIST

RATE THIS ACTIVITY

☆☆☆☆☆

I WANT TO DO THIS BECAUSE...

_____

_____

_____

_____

MAKE IT HAPPEN: HOW? WHEN?

_____

_____

_____

_____

REVIEW

DATE COMPLETED: /   /

_____

WHAT HAPPENED? (PEOPLE MET, HIGH POINTS, CHALLENGES, EXPECTATIONS VS REALITY)

_____

_____

_____

_____

THE **BEST PART** WAS...

_____

_____

_____

_____

_____

BUDGET

$

ANTICIPATED DATE

/ /   TO   / /

ACTION LIST

⊘
⊘
⊘
⊘
⊘
⊘
⊘
⊘
⊘

SUCCESS! ✓

PLACE A CHECK HERE TO
TAKE IT OFF YOUR BUCKET LIST

RATE THIS ACTIVITY

☆☆☆☆☆

PRIORITY ☆☆☆☆☆　　ITEM #43: _____

I WANT TO DO THIS BECAUSE...

_____

_____

_____

_____

MAKE IT HAPPEN: HOW? WHEN?

_____

_____

_____

_____

REVIEW

DATE COMPLETED: 　 / /

WHAT HAPPENED? (PEOPLE MET, HIGH POINTS, CHALLENGES, EXPECTATIONS VS REALITY)

_____

_____

_____

_____

_____

THE **BEST PART** WAS...

_____

_____

_____

_____

_____

BUDGET

$

ANTICIPATED DATE

/ /　　TO　　/ /

ACTION LIST

- ⊘
- ⊘
- ⊘
- ⊘
- ⊘
- ⊘
- ⊘
- ⊘
- ⊘

SUCCESS!

✓

PLACE A CHECK HERE TO
TAKE IT OFF YOUR BUCKET LIST

RATE THIS ACTIVITY

☆☆☆☆☆

YOU KNOW YOU'RE GETTING OLD WHEN YOU STOOP TO TIE YOUR SHOELACES AND WONDER
WHAT ELSE YOU COULD DO WHILE YOU'RE DOWN THERE. GEORGE BURNS

ITEM #44: _____

I WANT TO DO THIS BECAUSE...

_____
_____
_____
_____

MAKE IT HAPPEN: HOW? WHEN?

_____
_____
_____
_____

REVIEW

DATE COMPLETED: /   /

WHAT HAPPENED? (PEOPLE MET, HIGH POINTS, CHALLENGES, EXPECTATIONS VS REALITY)

_____
_____
_____
_____
_____

THE **BEST PART** WAS...

_____
_____
_____
_____
_____

BUDGET

$

ANTICIPATED DATE

/ /   TO   / /

ACTION LIST

⊘
⊘
⊘
⊘
⊘
⊘
⊘
⊘
⊘

SUCCESS! ✓

PLACE A CHECK HERE TO
TAKE IT OFF YOUR BUCKET LIST

RATE THIS ACTIVITY

☆☆☆☆☆

PEOPLE ASK ME WHAT I'D MOST APPRECIATE GETTING FOR MY EIGHTY-SEVENTH BIRTHDAY; I TELL THEM, A PATERNITY SUIT. GEORGE BURNS

PRIORITY ☆☆☆☆☆   ITEM #45: _____

I WANT TO DO THIS BECAUSE...	**BUDGET**
	$

MAKE IT HAPPEN: HOW? WHEN?

ANTICIPATED DATE

/ /   TO   / /

ACTION LIST

⊘
⊘
⊘
⊘
⊘
⊘
⊘
⊘
⊘

REVIEW

DATE COMPLETED: / /

WHAT HAPPENED? (PEOPLE MET, HIGH POINTS, CHALLENGES, EXPECTATIONS VS REALITY)

SUCCESS! ✓

PLACE A CHECK HERE TO
TAKE IT OFF YOUR BUCKET LIST

THE **BEST PART** WAS...

RATE THIS ACTIVITY

☆☆☆☆☆

ITEM #46: _____

I WANT TO DO THIS BECAUSE...	**BUDGET**
	$

ANTICIPATED DATE

/ /   TO   / /

MAKE IT HAPPEN: HOW? WHEN?

ACTION LIST

⊘
⊘
⊘
⊘
⊘
⊘
⊘
⊘
⊘

REVIEW

DATE COMPLETED: / /

WHAT HAPPENED? (PEOPLE MET, HIGH POINTS, CHALLENGES, EXPECTATIONS VS REALITY)

SUCCESS! ✓

PLACE A CHECK HERE TO
TAKE IT OFF YOUR BUCKET LIST

THE **BEST PART** WAS...

RATE THIS ACTIVITY

☆☆☆☆☆

ITEM #47: _____

I WANT TO DO THIS BECAUSE...

_____

_____

_____

_____

MAKE IT HAPPEN: HOW? WHEN?

_____

_____

_____

_____

REVIEW

DATE COMPLETED: / /

WHAT HAPPENED? (PEOPLE MET, HIGH POINTS, CHALLENGES, EXPECTATIONS VS REALITY)

_____

_____

_____

_____

THE **BEST PART** WAS...

_____

_____

_____

_____

_____

BUDGET

$

ANTICIPATED DATE

/ /   TO   / /

ACTION LIST

⊘
⊘
⊘
⊘
⊘
⊘
⊘
⊘
⊘

SUCCESS! ✓

PLACE A CHECK HERE TO
TAKE IT OFF YOUR BUCKET LIST

RATE THIS ACTIVITY

☆☆☆☆☆

I WANT TO DO THIS BECAUSE...

BUDGET

$

ANTICIPATED DATE

/ /   TO   / /

MAKE IT HAPPEN: HOW? WHEN?

ACTION LIST

⊘
⊘
⊘
⊘
⊘
⊘
⊘
⊘
⊘

REVIEW

DATE COMPLETED: / /

WHAT HAPPENED? (PEOPLE MET, HIGH POINTS, CHALLENGES, EXPECTATIONS VS REALITY)

SUCCESS! ✓

PLACE A CHECK HERE TO
TAKE IT OFF YOUR BUCKET LIST

THE **BEST PART** WAS...

RATE THIS ACTIVITY

☆☆☆☆☆

ITEM #49: _____

I WANT TO DO THIS BECAUSE...

MAKE IT HAPPEN: HOW? WHEN?

REVIEW

DATE COMPLETED: /   /

WHAT HAPPENED? (PEOPLE MET, HIGH POINTS, CHALLENGES, EXPECTATIONS VS REALITY)

THE **BEST PART** WAS...

BUDGET

$

ANTICIPATED DATE

/ /   TO   / /

ACTION LIST

- ⊘
- ⊘
- ⊘
- ⊘
- ⊘
- ⊘
- ⊘
- ⊘
- ⊘
- ⊘

SUCCESS! ✓

PLACE A CHECK HERE TO
TAKE IT OFF YOUR BUCKET LIST

RATE THIS ACTIVITY

☆☆☆☆☆

I WANT TO DO THIS BECAUSE...

_____
_____
_____
_____

MAKE IT HAPPEN: HOW? WHEN?

_____
_____
_____
_____

REVIEW

DATE COMPLETED: /   /

WHAT HAPPENED? (PEOPLE MET, HIGH POINTS, CHALLENGES, EXPECTATIONS VS REALITY)

_____
_____
_____
_____

THE **BEST PART** WAS...

_____
_____
_____
_____
_____
_____

BUDGET

$

ANTICIPATED DATE

/   /   TO   /   /

ACTION LIST

⊘
⊘
⊘
⊘
⊘
⊘
⊘
⊘
⊘

SUCCESS! ✓

PLACE A CHECK HERE TO
TAKE IT OFF YOUR BUCKET LIST

RATE THIS ACTIVITY

☆☆☆☆☆

I WANT TO DO THIS BECAUSE...

MAKE IT HAPPEN: HOW? WHEN?

REVIEW

DATE COMPLETED: / /

WHAT HAPPENED? (PEOPLE MET, HIGH POINTS, CHALLENGES, EXPECTATIONS VS REALITY)

THE **BEST PART** WAS...

BUDGET

$

ANTICIPATED DATE

/ /   TO   / /

ACTION LIST

○
○
○
○
○
○
○
○
○

SUCCESS!

PLACE A CHECK HERE TO
TAKE IT OFF YOUR BUCKET LIST

RATE THIS ACTIVITY

☆☆☆☆☆

I WANT TO DO THIS BECAUSE...

_____

_____

_____

_____

MAKE IT HAPPEN: HOW? WHEN?

_____

_____

_____

_____

REVIEW

DATE COMPLETED: / /

WHAT HAPPENED? (PEOPLE MET, HIGH POINTS, CHALLENGES, EXPECTATIONS VS REALITY)

_____

_____

_____

_____

THE **BEST PART** WAS...

_____

_____

_____

_____

_____

BUDGET

$

ANTICIPATED DATE

/ /   TO   / /

ACTION LIST

⊘ _____
⊘ _____
⊘ _____
⊘ _____
⊘ _____
⊘ _____
⊘ _____
⊘ _____
⊘ _____

SUCCESS! ✓

PLACE A CHECK HERE TO
TAKE IT OFF YOUR BUCKET LIST

RATE THIS ACTIVITY

☆☆☆☆☆

PRIORITY ☆☆☆☆☆   ITEM #53: _____

I WANT TO DO THIS BECAUSE...	**BUDGET**
	$
	ANTICIPATED DATE
	/ / TO / /
MAKE IT HAPPEN: HOW? WHEN?	**ACTION LIST**
	⊘
	⊘
	⊘
	⊘
	⊘
	⊘
	⊘

REVIEW

DATE COMPLETED: / /

WHAT HAPPENED? (PEOPLE MET, HIGH POINTS, CHALLENGES, EXPECTATIONS VS REALITY)

SUCCESS!

PLACE A CHECK HERE TO
TAKE IT OFF YOUR BUCKET LIST

THE **BEST PART** WAS...

RATE THIS ACTIVITY

☆☆☆☆☆

I WANT TO DO THIS BECAUSE...

MAKE IT HAPPEN: HOW? WHEN?

REVIEW

DATE COMPLETED: / /

WHAT HAPPENED? (PEOPLE MET, HIGH POINTS, CHALLENGES, EXPECTATIONS VS REALITY)

THE **BEST PART** WAS...

BUDGET

$

ANTICIPATED DATE

/ /   TO   / /

ACTION LIST

- ⊘
- ⊘
- ⊘
- ⊘
- ⊘
- ⊘
- ⊘
- ⊘
- ⊘

SUCCESS!

PLACE A CHECK HERE TO
TAKE IT OFF YOUR BUCKET LIST

RATE THIS ACTIVITY

☆☆☆☆☆

PRIORITY ☆☆☆☆☆   ITEM #55: _____

I WANT TO DO THIS BECAUSE...

_____

_____

_____

_____

MAKE IT HAPPEN: HOW? WHEN?

_____

_____

_____

_____

REVIEW

DATE COMPLETED: /   /

WHAT HAPPENED? (PEOPLE MET, HIGH POINTS, CHALLENGES, EXPECTATIONS VS REALITY)

_____

_____

_____

_____

THE **BEST PART** WAS...

_____

_____

_____

_____

_____

BUDGET

$

ANTICIPATED DATE

/   /   TO   /   /

ACTION LIST

⊘
⊘
⊘
⊘
⊘
⊘
⊘
⊘
⊘

SUCCESS!

✓

PLACE A CHECK HERE TO
TAKE IT OFF YOUR BUCKET LIST

RATE THIS ACTIVITY

☆☆☆☆☆

I WANT TO DO THIS BECAUSE...

_____

_____

_____

MAKE IT HAPPEN: HOW? WHEN?

_____

_____

_____

_____

REVIEW

DATE COMPLETED: / /

WHAT HAPPENED? (PEOPLE MET, HIGH POINTS, CHALLENGES,
EXPECTATIONS VS REALITY)

_____

_____

_____

_____

THE **BEST PART** WAS...

_____

_____

_____

_____

_____

_____

BUDGET

$

ANTICIPATED DATE

/ /   TO   / /

ACTION LIST

- ⊘
- ⊘
- ⊘
- ⊘
- ⊘
- ⊘
- ⊘
- ⊘
- ⊘

SUCCESS! ✓

PLACE A CHECK HERE TO
TAKE IT OFF YOUR BUCKET LIST

RATE THIS ACTIVITY

☆☆☆☆☆

AT AGE 20, WE WORRY ABOUT WHAT OTHERS THINK OF US; AT AGE 40, WE DON'T CARE WHAT THEY THINK
OF US; AT AGE 60, WE DISCOVER THEY HAVEN'T BEEN THINKING OF US AT ALL. ANN LANDERS

I WANT TO DO THIS BECAUSE...

_____

_____

MAKE IT HAPPEN: HOW? WHEN?

_____

_____

_____

REVIEW

DATE COMPLETED: / /

WHAT HAPPENED? (PEOPLE MET, HIGH POINTS, CHALLENGES, EXPECTATIONS VS REALITY)

_____

_____

_____

THE **BEST PART** WAS...

_____

_____

BUDGET

$

ANTICIPATED DATE

/ /   TO   / /

ACTION LIST

- ◯
- ◯
- ◯
- ◯
- ◯
- ◯
- ◯
- ◯
- ◯

SUCCESS! ✓

PLACE A CHECK HERE TO
TAKE IT OFF YOUR BUCKET LIST

RATE THIS ACTIVITY

☆☆☆☆☆

PREPARATION FOR OLD AGE SHOULD BEGIN NOT LATER THAN ONE'S TEENS; A LIFE WHICH IS EMPTY OF
PURPOSE UNTIL 65 WILL NOT SUDDENLY BECOME FILLED ON RETIREMENT. ARTHUR E. MORGAN

57

I WANT TO DO THIS BECAUSE...

_____

_____

_____

MAKE IT HAPPEN: HOW? WHEN?

_____

_____

_____

REVIEW

DATE COMPLETED: / /

WHAT HAPPENED? (PEOPLE MET, HIGH POINTS, CHALLENGES, EXPECTATIONS VS REALITY)

_____

_____

_____

_____

THE **BEST PART** WAS...

_____

_____

_____

_____

BUDGET

$

ANTICIPATED DATE

/ /   TO   / /

ACTION LIST

- ⊘
- ⊘
- ⊘
- ⊘
- ⊘
- ⊘
- ⊘
- ⊘
- ⊘

SUCCESS! ✓

PLACE A CHECK HERE TO
TAKE IT OFF YOUR BUCKET LIST

RATE THIS ACTIVITY

☆☆☆☆☆

BEFORE YOU SPEAK, LISTEN; BEFORE YOU WRITE, THINK; BEFORE YOU SPEND, EARN; BEFORE YOU INVEST, INVESTIGATE; BEFORE YOU CRITICIZE, WAIT; BEFORE YOU PRAY, FORGIVE; BEFORE YOU QUIT, TRY; BEFORE YOU RETIRE, SAVE; BEFORE YOU DIE, GIVE. WILLIAM A. WARD

ITEM #59: _____

I WANT TO DO THIS BECAUSE...

_____

_____

_____

_____

MAKE IT HAPPEN: HOW? WHEN?

_____

_____

_____

_____

_____

REVIEW

DATE COMPLETED: / /

_____

WHAT HAPPENED? (PEOPLE MET, HIGH POINTS, CHALLENGES, EXPECTATIONS VS REALITY)

_____

_____

_____

_____

_____

THE **BEST PART** WAS...

_____

_____

_____

_____

_____

_____

BUDGET

$

ANTICIPATED DATE

/ /   TO   / /

ACTION LIST

⊘
⊘
⊘
⊘
⊘
⊘
⊘
⊘
⊘

SUCCESS! ✓

PLACE A CHECK HERE TO
TAKE IT OFF YOUR BUCKET LIST

RATE THIS ACTIVITY

☆☆☆☆☆

I WANT TO DO THIS BECAUSE...

_____
_____
_____
_____

MAKE IT HAPPEN: HOW? WHEN?

_____
_____
_____
_____

REVIEW

DATE COMPLETED: ___ / ___ / ___

WHAT HAPPENED? (PEOPLE MET, HIGH POINTS, CHALLENGES, EXPECTATIONS VS REALITY)

_____
_____
_____
_____

THE **BEST PART** WAS...

_____
_____
_____
_____
_____

BUDGET

$

ANTICIPATED DATE

___ / ___　TO　___ / ___

ACTION LIST

- ⊘
- ⊘
- ⊘
- ⊘
- ⊘
- ⊘
- ⊘
- ⊘
- ⊘

SUCCESS! ✓

PLACE A CHECK HERE TO
TAKE IT OFF YOUR BUCKET LIST

RATE THIS ACTIVITY

☆☆☆☆☆

RETIREMENT IS LIKE A LONG VACATION IN LAS VEGAS; THE GOAL IS TO ENJOY IT THE FULLEST,
BUT NOT SO FULLY THAT YOU RUN OUT OF MONEY. JONATHAN CLEMENTS

ITEM #61: _____

I WANT TO DO THIS BECAUSE...

_____

_____

_____

_____

MAKE IT HAPPEN: HOW? WHEN?

_____

_____

_____

_____

_____

REVIEW

DATE COMPLETED: /   /

WHAT HAPPENED? (PEOPLE MET, HIGH POINTS, CHALLENGES, EXPECTATIONS VS REALITY)

_____

_____

_____

_____

_____

THE **BEST PART** WAS...

_____

_____

_____

_____

_____

BUDGET

$

ANTICIPATED DATE

/ /   TO   / /

ACTION LIST

- ⊘
- ⊘
- ⊘
- ⊘
- ⊘
- ⊘
- ⊘
- ⊘
- ⊘

SUCCESS!

✓

PLACE A CHECK HERE TO
TAKE IT OFF YOUR BUCKET LIST

RATE THIS ACTIVITY

☆☆☆☆☆

IT IS BETTER TO LIVE RICH THAN TO DIE RICH. SAMUEL JOHNSON

I WANT TO DO THIS BECAUSE...

MAKE IT HAPPEN: HOW? WHEN?

REVIEW

DATE COMPLETED: / /

WHAT HAPPENED? (PEOPLE MET, HIGH POINTS, CHALLENGES, EXPECTATIONS VS REALITY)

THE **BEST PART** WAS...

BUDGET

$

ANTICIPATED DATE

/ / TO / /

ACTION LIST

- ⊘
- ⊘
- ⊘
- ⊘
- ⊘
- ⊘
- ⊘
- ⊘
- ⊘

SUCCESS! ✓

PLACE A CHECK HERE TO
TAKE IT OFF YOUR BUCKET LIST

RATE THIS ACTIVITY

☆☆☆☆☆

I WANT TO DO THIS BECAUSE...

_____

_____

_____

_____

MAKE IT HAPPEN: HOW? WHEN?

_____

_____

_____

_____

_____

REVIEW

DATE COMPLETED: / /

WHAT HAPPENED? (PEOPLE MET, HIGH POINTS, CHALLENGES, EXPECTATIONS VS REALITY)

_____

_____

_____

_____

_____

THE **BEST PART** WAS...

_____

_____

_____

_____

_____

BUDGET

$

ANTICIPATED DATE

/ /   TO   / /

ACTION LIST

⊘
⊘
⊘
⊘
⊘
⊘
⊘
⊘
⊘

SUCCESS! ✓

PLACE A CHECK HERE TO
TAKE IT OFF YOUR BUCKET LIST

RATE THIS ACTIVITY

☆☆☆☆☆

I WANT TO DO THIS BECAUSE...

MAKE IT HAPPEN: HOW? WHEN?

REVIEW

DATE COMPLETED: / /

WHAT HAPPENED? (PEOPLE MET, HIGH POINTS, CHALLENGES, EXPECTATIONS VS REALITY)

THE **BEST PART** WAS...

BUDGET

$

ANTICIPATED DATE

/ /   TO   / /

ACTION LIST

⊘
⊘
⊘
⊘
⊘
⊘
⊘
⊘
⊘

SUCCESS! ✓

PLACE A CHECK HERE TO
TAKE IT OFF YOUR BUCKET LIST

RATE THIS ACTIVITY

☆☆☆☆☆

ITEM #65: _____

I WANT TO DO THIS BECAUSE...

MAKE IT HAPPEN: HOW? WHEN?

REVIEW

DATE COMPLETED: /   /

WHAT HAPPENED? (PEOPLE MET, HIGH POINTS, CHALLENGES, EXPECTATIONS VS REALITY)

THE **BEST PART** WAS...

BUDGET

$

ANTICIPATED DATE

/ /   TO   / /

ACTION LIST

- ⊘
- ⊘
- ⊘
- ⊘
- ⊘
- ⊘
- ⊘
- ⊘
- ⊘

SUCCESS! ✓

PLACE A CHECK HERE TO
TAKE IT OFF YOUR BUCKET LIST

RATE THIS ACTIVITY

☆☆☆☆☆

I WANT TO DO THIS BECAUSE...

_____

_____

_____

MAKE IT HAPPEN: HOW? WHEN?

_____

_____

_____

REVIEW

DATE COMPLETED: / /

WHAT HAPPENED? (PEOPLE MET, HIGH POINTS, CHALLENGES, EXPECTATIONS VS REALITY)

_____

_____

_____

_____

THE **BEST PART** WAS...

_____

_____

_____

_____

BUDGET

$

ANTICIPATED DATE

/ /   TO   / /

ACTION LIST

- ⊘
- ⊘
- ⊘
- ⊘
- ⊘
- ⊘
- ⊘
- ⊘
- ⊘

SUCCESS! ✓

PLACE A CHECK HERE TO
TAKE IT OFF YOUR BUCKET LIST

RATE THIS ACTIVITY

☆☆☆☆☆

PRIORITY ☆☆☆☆☆

ITEM #67: _____

I WANT TO DO THIS BECAUSE...

MAKE IT HAPPEN: HOW? WHEN?

REVIEW

DATE COMPLETED: / /

WHAT HAPPENED? (PEOPLE MET, HIGH POINTS, CHALLENGES, EXPECTATIONS VS REALITY)

THE **BEST PART** WAS...

BUDGET

$

ANTICIPATED DATE

/ /   TO   / /

ACTION LIST

- ⊘
- ⊘
- ⊘
- ⊘
- ⊘
- ⊘
- ⊘
- ⊘
- ⊘

SUCCESS!

PLACE A CHECK HERE TO
TAKE IT OFF YOUR BUCKET LIST

RATE THIS ACTIVITY

☆☆☆☆☆

I WANT TO DO THIS BECAUSE...

_____

_____

_____

MAKE IT HAPPEN: HOW? WHEN?

_____

_____

_____

REVIEW

DATE COMPLETED: / /

WHAT HAPPENED? (PEOPLE MET, HIGH POINTS, CHALLENGES, EXPECTATIONS VS REALITY)

_____

_____

_____

_____

THE **BEST PART** WAS...

_____

_____

_____

_____

BUDGET

$

ANTICIPATED DATE

/ / TO / /

ACTION LIST

- ⊘
- ⊘
- ⊘
- ⊘
- ⊘
- ⊘
- ⊘
- ⊘
- ⊘

SUCCESS!

PLACE A CHECK HERE TO
TAKE IT OFF YOUR BUCKET LIST

RATE THIS ACTIVITY

☆☆☆☆☆

PRIORITY ☆☆☆☆☆

ITEM #69: _____

I WANT TO DO THIS BECAUSE...

_____
_____
_____
_____

MAKE IT HAPPEN: HOW? WHEN?

_____
_____
_____
_____

REVIEW

DATE COMPLETED: / /

_____

WHAT HAPPENED? (PEOPLE MET, HIGH POINTS, CHALLENGES, EXPECTATIONS VS REALITY)

_____
_____
_____
_____

THE **BEST PART** WAS...

_____
_____
_____
_____

BUDGET

$

ANTICIPATED DATE

/ /   TO   / /

ACTION LIST

○
○
○
○
○
○
○
○
○

SUCCESS! ✓

PLACE A CHECK HERE TO
TAKE IT OFF YOUR BUCKET LIST

RATE THIS ACTIVITY

☆☆☆☆☆

RETIREMENT'S THE MOST WONDERFUL THING; I GET TO ENJOY ALL THE THINGS I NEVER STOPPED TO NOTICE ON THE WAY UP; AFTER AN EXTRAORDINARY LIFE, IT'S TIME TO ENJOY MY RETIREMENT. PATRICK MACNEE

69

I WANT TO DO THIS BECAUSE...

BUDGET

$

ANTICIPATED DATE

/ /   TO   / /

MAKE IT HAPPEN: HOW? WHEN?

ACTION LIST

REVIEW

DATE COMPLETED: / /

WHAT HAPPENED? (PEOPLE MET, HIGH POINTS, CHALLENGES, EXPECTATIONS VS REALITY)

SUCCESS!

PLACE A CHECK HERE TO
TAKE IT OFF YOUR BUCKET LIST

THE **BEST PART** WAS...

RATE THIS ACTIVITY

☆☆☆☆☆

I FOUND OUT RETIREMENT MEANS PLAYING GOLF, OR I DON'T KNOW WHAT THE HELL IT MEANS; BUT
TO ME, RETIREMENT MEANS DOING WHAT YOU HAVE FUN DOING. DICK VAN DYKE

I WANT TO DO THIS BECAUSE...

_____

_____

_____

MAKE IT HAPPEN: HOW? WHEN?

_____

_____

_____

REVIEW

DATE COMPLETED: / /

WHAT HAPPENED? (PEOPLE MET, HIGH POINTS, CHALLENGES, EXPECTATIONS VS REALITY)

_____

_____

_____

_____

THE **BEST PART** WAS...

_____

_____

_____

BUDGET

$

ANTICIPATED DATE

/ /   TO   / /

ACTION LIST

⊘
⊘
⊘
⊘
⊘
⊘
⊘
⊘
⊘
⊘

SUCCESS! ✓

PLACE A CHECK HERE TO
TAKE IT OFF YOUR BUCKET LIST

RATE THIS ACTIVITY

☆☆☆☆☆

WE WORK ALL OUR LIVES SO WE CAN RETIRE – SO WE CAN DO WHAT WE WANT WITH OUR TIME – AND THE
WAY WE DEFINE OR SPEND OUR TIME DEFINES WHO WE ARE AND WHAT WE VALUE. BRUCE LINTON

71

ITEM #72: _____

I WANT TO DO THIS BECAUSE...	**BUDGET**

$ _____

ANTICIPATED DATE

/ /   TO   / /

MAKE IT HAPPEN: HOW? WHEN?

ACTION LIST

- ⊘
- ⊘
- ⊘
- ⊘
- ⊘
- ⊘
- ⊘
- ⊘
- ⊘

REVIEW

DATE COMPLETED: / /

WHAT HAPPENED? (PEOPLE MET, HIGH POINTS, CHALLENGES, EXPECTATIONS VS REALITY)

SUCCESS!

✓

PLACE A CHECK HERE TO
TAKE IT OFF YOUR BUCKET LIST

RATE THIS ACTIVITY

☆☆☆☆☆

THE **BEST PART** WAS...

THE JOY OF RETIREMENT COMES IN THOSE EVERYDAY PURSUITS THAT EMBRACE THE JOY OF LIFE; TO EXPERIENCE DAILY
THE FREEDOM TO INVEST ONE'S LIFE-LONG KNOWLEDGE FOR THE BETTERMENT OF OTHERS; AND, TO ALLOCATE TIME
TO PURSUITS THAT ONLY RECEIVED, IN YEARS OF WORKING, A FLEETING MOMENT. BYRON PULSIFER

PRIORITY ☆☆☆☆☆

ITEM #73: _____

I WANT TO DO THIS BECAUSE...

_____
_____
_____
_____

MAKE IT HAPPEN: HOW? WHEN?

_____
_____
_____
_____

REVIEW

DATE COMPLETED: /   /

WHAT HAPPENED? (PEOPLE MET, HIGH POINTS, CHALLENGES, EXPECTATIONS VS REALITY)

_____
_____
_____
_____
_____

THE **BEST PART** WAS...

_____
_____
_____
_____
_____
_____

BUDGET

$

ANTICIPATED DATE

/ /   TO   / /

ACTION LIST

- ⊘
- ⊘
- ⊘
- ⊘
- ⊘
- ⊘
- ⊘
- ⊘
- ⊘

SUCCESS! ✓

PLACE A CHECK HERE TO
TAKE IT OFF YOUR BUCKET LIST

RATE THIS ACTIVITY

☆☆☆☆☆

A THRIVING NEW BEGINNING CAN BE AND SHOULD BE A TIME FOR AMAZING ENGAGEMENT, GROWTH, CONNECTIONS, CONTRIBUTIONS, AND AMAZING POSSIBILITIES. LEE M. BROWER

73

I WANT TO DO THIS BECAUSE...

_____
_____
_____
_____

MAKE IT HAPPEN: HOW? WHEN?

_____
_____
_____
_____

REVIEW

DATE COMPLETED: / /

WHAT HAPPENED? (PEOPLE MET, HIGH POINTS, CHALLENGES, EXPECTATIONS VS REALITY)

_____
_____
_____
_____
_____

THE **BEST PART** WAS...

_____
_____
_____
_____
_____

BUDGET

$

ANTICIPATED DATE

/ / TO / /

ACTION LIST

- ⊘
- ⊘
- ⊘
- ⊘
- ⊘
- ⊘
- ⊘
- ⊘
- ⊘

SUCCESS! ✓

PLACE A CHECK HERE TO
TAKE IT OFF YOUR BUCKET LIST

RATE THIS ACTIVITY

☆☆☆☆☆

AS YOUR LIFE CHANGES, IT TAKES TIME TO RECALIBRATE, TO FIND YOUR VALUES AGAIN; YOU MIGHT ALSO FIND THAT
RETIREMENT IS THE TIME WHEN YOU STRETCH OUT AND FIND YOUR POTENTIAL. SID MIRAMONTES

I WANT TO DO THIS BECAUSE...

_____

_____

_____

_____

MAKE IT HAPPEN: HOW? WHEN?

_____

_____

_____

_____

REVIEW

DATE COMPLETED: / /

WHAT HAPPENED? (PEOPLE MET, HIGH POINTS, CHALLENGES, EXPECTATIONS VS REALITY)

_____

_____

_____

_____

THE **BEST PART** WAS...

_____

_____

_____

_____

BUDGET

$

ANTICIPATED DATE

/ /   TO   / /

ACTION LIST

- ⊘
- ⊘
- ⊘
- ⊘
- ⊘
- ⊘
- ⊘
- ⊘
- ⊘

SUCCESS! ✓

PLACE A CHECK HERE TO
TAKE IT OFF YOUR BUCKET LIST

RATE THIS ACTIVITY

☆☆☆☆☆

RETIREMENT, A TIME TO DO WHAT YOU WANT TO DO, WHEN YOU WANT TO DO IT, WHERE YOU
WANT TO DO IT AND HOW YOU WANT TO DO IT. CATHERINE PULSIFER

75

ITEM #76: _____

I WANT TO DO THIS BECAUSE...

_____

_____

_____

_____

MAKE IT HAPPEN: HOW? WHEN?

_____

_____

_____

_____

REVIEW

DATE COMPLETED: / /

WHAT HAPPENED? (PEOPLE MET, HIGH POINTS, CHALLENGES, EXPECTATIONS VS REALITY)

_____

_____

_____

_____

THE **BEST PART** WAS...

_____

_____

_____

_____

BUDGET

$

ANTICIPATED DATE

/ /   TO   / /

ACTION LIST

⊘ _____
⊘ _____
⊘ _____
⊘ _____
⊘ _____
⊘ _____
⊘ _____
⊘ _____
⊘ _____

SUCCESS! ✓

PLACE A CHECK HERE TO
TAKE IT OFF YOUR BUCKET LIST

RATE THIS ACTIVITY

☆☆☆☆☆

I WANT TO DO THIS BECAUSE...

MAKE IT HAPPEN: HOW? WHEN?

REVIEW

DATE COMPLETED: /   / .

WHAT HAPPENED? (PEOPLE MET, HIGH POINTS, CHALLENGES, EXPECTATIONS VS REALITY)

THE **BEST PART** WAS...

BUDGET

$

ANTICIPATED DATE

/ /   TO   / /

ACTION LIST

○
○
○
○
○
○
○
○
○

SUCCESS!

✓

PLACE A CHECK HERE TO
TAKE IT OFF YOUR BUCKET LIST

RATE THIS ACTIVITY

☆☆☆☆☆

I WANT TO DO THIS BECAUSE...

_____
_____
_____
_____

MAKE IT HAPPEN: HOW? WHEN?

_____
_____
_____
_____

REVIEW

DATE COMPLETED: / /

_____

WHAT HAPPENED? (PEOPLE MET, HIGH POINTS, CHALLENGES, EXPECTATIONS VS REALITY)

_____
_____
_____
_____
_____

THE **BEST PART** WAS...

_____
_____
_____
_____

BUDGET

$

ANTICIPATED DATE

/ /   TO   / /

ACTION LIST

- ⊘
- ⊘
- ⊘
- ⊘
- ⊘
- ⊘
- ⊘
- ⊘
- ⊘

SUCCESS!

✓

PLACE A CHECK HERE TO
TAKE IT OFF YOUR BUCKET LIST

RATE THIS ACTIVITY

☆☆☆☆☆

I WANT TO DO THIS BECAUSE...

MAKE IT HAPPEN: HOW? WHEN?

REVIEW

DATE COMPLETED: / /

WHAT HAPPENED? (PEOPLE MET, HIGH POINTS, CHALLENGES, EXPECTATIONS VS REALITY)

THE **BEST PART** WAS...

BUDGET

$

ANTICIPATED DATE

/ /   TO   / /

ACTION LIST

- ⊘
- ⊘
- ⊘
- ⊘
- ⊘
- ⊘
- ⊘
- ⊘
- ⊘

SUCCESS!

PLACE A CHECK HERE TO
TAKE IT OFF YOUR BUCKET LIST

RATE THIS ACTIVITY

☆☆☆☆☆

I WANT TO DO THIS BECAUSE...

_____

_____

_____

MAKE IT HAPPEN: HOW? WHEN?

_____

_____

_____

_____

REVIEW

DATE COMPLETED: / /

WHAT HAPPENED? (PEOPLE MET, HIGH POINTS, CHALLENGES, EXPECTATIONS VS REALITY)

_____

_____

_____

_____

THE **BEST PART** WAS...

_____

_____

_____

_____

BUDGET

$

ANTICIPATED DATE

/ /   TO   / /

ACTION LIST

- ⊘
- ⊘
- ⊘
- ⊘
- ⊘
- ⊘
- ⊘
- ⊘
- ⊘

SUCCESS! ✓

PLACE A CHECK HERE TO
TAKE IT OFF YOUR BUCKET LIST

RATE THIS ACTIVITY

☆☆☆☆☆

I WANT TO DO THIS BECAUSE...

_____
_____
_____
_____

MAKE IT HAPPEN: HOW? WHEN?

_____
_____
_____
_____

REVIEW

DATE COMPLETED: / /

WHAT HAPPENED? (PEOPLE MET, HIGH POINTS, CHALLENGES, EXPECTATIONS VS REALITY)

_____
_____
_____
_____
_____
_____

THE **BEST PART** WAS...

_____
_____
_____
_____
_____

BUDGET

$

ANTICIPATED DATE

/ / TO / /

ACTION LIST

○
○
○
○
○
○
○
○
○

SUCCESS!

PLACE A CHECK HERE TO
TAKE IT OFF YOUR BUCKET LIST

RATE THIS ACTIVITY

☆☆☆☆☆

PRIORITY ☆☆☆☆☆   ITEM #82:

I WANT TO DO THIS BECAUSE...

MAKE IT HAPPEN: HOW? WHEN?

REVIEW

DATE COMPLETED: / /

WHAT HAPPENED? (PEOPLE MET, HIGH POINTS, CHALLENGES, EXPECTATIONS VS REALITY)

THE **BEST PART** WAS...

BUDGET

$

ANTICIPATED DATE

/ /   TO   / /

ACTION LIST

- ⊘
- ⊘
- ⊘
- ⊘
- ⊘
- ⊘
- ⊘
- ⊘
- ⊘

SUCCESS! ✓

PLACE A CHECK HERE TO
TAKE IT OFF YOUR BUCKET LIST

RATE THIS ACTIVITY

☆☆☆☆☆

OFTEN WHEN YOU THINK YOU'RE AT THE END OF SOMETHING, YOU'RE AT THE BEGINNING OF SOMETHING ELSE. FRED ROGERS

I WANT TO DO THIS BECAUSE...

MAKE IT HAPPEN: HOW? WHEN?

REVIEW

DATE COMPLETED: /   /

WHAT HAPPENED? (PEOPLE MET, HIGH POINTS, CHALLENGES, EXPECTATIONS VS REALITY)

THE **BEST PART** WAS...

BUDGET

$

ANTICIPATED DATE

/ /   TO   / /

ACTION LIST

⊘
⊘
⊘
⊘
⊘
⊘
⊘
⊘
⊘

SUCCESS!

PLACE A CHECK HERE TO
TAKE IT OFF YOUR BUCKET LIST

RATE THIS ACTIVITY

☆☆☆☆☆

I WANT TO DO THIS BECAUSE...

_____

_____

_____

MAKE IT HAPPEN: HOW? WHEN?

_____

_____

_____

_____

REVIEW

DATE COMPLETED: / /

WHAT HAPPENED? (PEOPLE MET, HIGH POINTS, CHALLENGES, EXPECTATIONS VS REALITY)

_____

_____

_____

_____

THE **BEST PART** WAS...

_____

_____

_____

_____

BUDGET

$

ANTICIPATED DATE

/ /   TO   / /

ACTION LIST

- ⊘
- ⊘
- ⊘
- ⊘
- ⊘
- ⊘
- ⊘
- ⊘
- ⊘

SUCCESS! ✓

PLACE A CHECK HERE TO
TAKE IT OFF YOUR BUCKET LIST

RATE THIS ACTIVITY

☆☆☆☆☆

I WANT TO DO THIS BECAUSE...

_____

_____

_____

MAKE IT HAPPEN: HOW? WHEN?

_____

_____

_____

_____

REVIEW

DATE COMPLETED: / /

WHAT HAPPENED? (PEOPLE MET, HIGH POINTS, CHALLENGES, EXPECTATIONS VS REALITY)

_____

_____

_____

_____

THE **BEST PART** WAS...

_____

_____

_____

_____

BUDGET

$

ANTICIPATED DATE

/ /   TO   / /

ACTION LIST

- ⊘
- ⊘
- ⊘
- ⊘
- ⊘
- ⊘
- ⊘
- ⊘
- ⊘

SUCCESS! ✓

PLACE A CHECK HERE TO
TAKE IT OFF YOUR BUCKET LIST

RATE THIS ACTIVITY

☆☆☆☆☆

I WANT TO DO THIS BECAUSE...

BUDGET

$

ANTICIPATED DATE

/ /   TO   / /

MAKE IT HAPPEN: HOW? WHEN?

ACTION LIST

⊘ _____
⊘ _____
⊘ _____
⊘ _____
⊘ _____
⊘ _____
⊘ _____
⊘ _____
⊘ _____

REVIEW

DATE COMPLETED: / /

WHAT HAPPENED? (PEOPLE MET, HIGH POINTS, CHALLENGES, EXPECTATIONS VS REALITY)

SUCCESS!

✓

PLACE A CHECK HERE TO
TAKE IT OFF YOUR BUCKET LIST

THE **BEST PART** WAS...

RATE THIS ACTIVITY

☆☆☆☆☆

ITEM #87: _____

I WANT TO DO THIS BECAUSE...

_____

_____

_____

_____

MAKE IT HAPPEN: HOW? WHEN?

_____

_____

_____

_____

_____

REVIEW

DATE COMPLETED: / /

WHAT HAPPENED? (PEOPLE MET, HIGH POINTS, CHALLENGES, EXPECTATIONS VS REALITY)

_____

_____

_____

_____

_____

THE **BEST PART** WAS...

_____

_____

_____

_____

BUDGET

$

ANTICIPATED DATE

/ /   TO   / /

ACTION LIST

⊘
⊘
⊘
⊘
⊘
⊘
⊘
⊘
⊘

SUCCESS!

PLACE A CHECK HERE TO
TAKE IT OFF YOUR BUCKET LIST

RATE THIS ACTIVITY

☆☆☆☆☆

MIDDLE AGE IS WHEN WORK IS A LOT LESS FUN AND FUN IS A LOT MORE WORK. ANONYMOUS

ITEM #88: _____

I WANT TO DO THIS BECAUSE...

MAKE IT HAPPEN: HOW? WHEN?

REVIEW

DATE COMPLETED: /   /

WHAT HAPPENED? (PEOPLE MET, HIGH POINTS, CHALLENGES, EXPECTATIONS VS REALITY)

THE **BEST PART** WAS...

BUDGET

$

ANTICIPATED DATE

/   /   TO   /   /

ACTION LIST

- ⊘
- ⊘
- ⊘
- ⊘
- ⊘
- ⊘
- ⊘
- ⊘
- ⊘

SUCCESS! ✓

PLACE A CHECK HERE TO
TAKE IT OFF YOUR BUCKET LIST

RATE THIS ACTIVITY

☆☆☆☆☆

REST IS NOT IDLENESS, AND TO LIE SOMETIMES ON THE GRASS UNDER TREES ON A SUMMER'S DAY, LISTENING TO THE MURMUR OF THE WATER, OR WATCHING THE CLOUDS FLOAT ACROSS THE SKY, IS BY NO MEANS A WASTE OF TIME. J. LUBBOCK

ITEM #89: _____

I WANT TO DO THIS BECAUSE...

_____

_____

_____

MAKE IT HAPPEN: HOW? WHEN?

_____

_____

_____

_____

REVIEW

DATE COMPLETED: ___ / ___ / ___

_____

WHAT HAPPENED? (PEOPLE MET, HIGH POINTS, CHALLENGES, EXPECTATIONS VS REALITY)

_____

_____

_____

_____

THE **BEST PART** WAS...

_____

_____

_____

BUDGET

$

ANTICIPATED DATE

___ / ___ TO ___ / ___

ACTION LIST

- ⊘
- ⊘
- ⊘
- ⊘
- ⊘
- ⊘
- ⊘
- ⊘
- ⊘

SUCCESS! ✓

PLACE A CHECK HERE TO
TAKE IT OFF YOUR BUCKET LIST

RATE THIS ACTIVITY

☆☆☆☆☆

I WANT TO DO THIS BECAUSE...

_____

_____

_____

_____

MAKE IT HAPPEN: HOW? WHEN?

_____

_____

_____

_____

_____

REVIEW

DATE COMPLETED: / /

_____

WHAT HAPPENED? (PEOPLE MET, HIGH POINTS, CHALLENGES, EXPECTATIONS VS REALITY)

_____

_____

_____

_____

_____

THE **BEST PART** WAS...

_____

_____

_____

_____

_____

BUDGET

$

ANTICIPATED DATE

/ /   TO   / /

ACTION LIST

○ _____
○ _____
○ _____
○ _____
○ _____
○ _____
○ _____
○ _____
○ _____

SUCCESS! ✓

PLACE A CHECK HERE TO
TAKE IT OFF YOUR BUCKET LIST

RATE THIS ACTIVITY

☆☆☆☆☆

PRIORITY ☆☆☆☆☆

ITEM #91: _____

I WANT TO DO THIS BECAUSE...
_____
_____
_____

MAKE IT HAPPEN: HOW? WHEN?
_____
_____
_____
_____

REVIEW

DATE COMPLETED: / /

WHAT HAPPENED? (PEOPLE MET, HIGH POINTS, CHALLENGES, EXPECTATIONS VS REALITY)
_____
_____
_____
_____

THE **BEST PART** WAS...
_____
_____
_____
_____

BUDGET

$

ANTICIPATED DATE

/ / TO / /

ACTION LIST

⊘
⊘
⊘
⊘
⊘
⊘
⊘
⊘
⊘

SUCCESS! ✓

PLACE A CHECK HERE TO
TAKE IT OFF YOUR BUCKET LIST

RATE THIS ACTIVITY

☆☆☆☆☆

I WANT TO DO THIS BECAUSE...

MAKE IT HAPPEN: HOW? WHEN?

REVIEW

DATE COMPLETED: / /

WHAT HAPPENED? (PEOPLE MET, HIGH POINTS, CHALLENGES, EXPECTATIONS VS REALITY)

THE **BEST PART** WAS...

BUDGET

$

ANTICIPATED DATE

/ /   TO   / /

ACTION LIST

- ⊘
- ⊘
- ⊘
- ⊘
- ⊘
- ⊘
- ⊘
- ⊘
- ⊘

SUCCESS! ✓

PLACE A CHECK HERE TO
TAKE IT OFF YOUR BUCKET LIST

RATE THIS ACTIVITY

☆☆☆☆☆

OUR LIFE, EXEMPT FROM PUBLIC HAUNT, FINDS TONGUES IN TREES, BOOKS IN THE RUNNING BROOKS,
SERMONS IN STONES, AND GOOD IN EVERYTHING. WILLIAM SHAKESPEARE

PRIORITY ☆☆☆☆☆

ITEM #93: _____

I WANT TO DO THIS BECAUSE...

_____
_____
_____

MAKE IT HAPPEN: HOW? WHEN?

_____
_____
_____
_____
_____

REVIEW

DATE COMPLETED: / /

WHAT HAPPENED? (PEOPLE MET, HIGH POINTS, CHALLENGES, EXPECTATIONS VS REALITY)

_____
_____
_____
_____

THE **BEST PART** WAS...

_____
_____
_____
_____
_____

BUDGET

$

ANTICIPATED DATE

/ /   TO   / /

ACTION LIST

⊘
⊘
⊘
⊘
⊘
⊘
⊘
⊘
⊘

SUCCESS!

✓

PLACE A CHECK HERE TO
TAKE IT OFF YOUR BUCKET LIST

RATE THIS ACTIVITY

☆☆☆☆☆

I WANT TO DO THIS BECAUSE...

BUDGET

$

ANTICIPATED DATE

/ /   TO   / /

MAKE IT HAPPEN: HOW? WHEN?

ACTION LIST

REVIEW

DATE COMPLETED: / /

WHAT HAPPENED? (PEOPLE MET, HIGH POINTS, CHALLENGES, EXPECTATIONS VS REALITY)

SUCCESS!

PLACE A CHECK HERE TO
TAKE IT OFF YOUR BUCKET LIST

THE **BEST PART** WAS...

RATE THIS ACTIVITY

☆☆☆☆☆

WHEN A MAN RETIRES, HIS WIFE GETS TWICE THE HUSBAND BUT ONLY HALF THE INCOME. CHI CHI RODRIGUEZ

ITEM #95: _____

I WANT TO DO THIS BECAUSE...

_____

_____

_____

_____

MAKE IT HAPPEN: HOW? WHEN?

_____

_____

_____

_____

REVIEW

DATE COMPLETED: / /

WHAT HAPPENED? (PEOPLE MET, HIGH POINTS, CHALLENGES, EXPECTATIONS VS REALITY)

_____

_____

_____

_____

THE **BEST PART** WAS...

_____

_____

_____

_____

_____

BUDGET

$

ANTICIPATED DATE

/ /   TO   / /

ACTION LIST

⊘
⊘
⊘
⊘
⊘
⊘
⊘
⊘
⊘

SUCCESS!

PLACE A CHECK HERE TO
TAKE IT OFF YOUR BUCKET LIST

RATE THIS ACTIVITY

☆☆☆☆☆

FEAR NO MORE THE HEAT O THE SUN, NOR THE FURIOUS WINTER'S RAGES; THOU THY WORLDLY TASK
HAST DONE, HOME ART GONE AND TAKEN THY WAGES. WILLIAM SHAKESPEARE

PRIORITY ☆☆☆☆☆   ITEM #96: _____

I WANT TO DO THIS BECAUSE...	**BUDGET**
	$

MAKE IT HAPPEN: HOW? WHEN?

/ / TO / /

ACTION LIST

⊘
⊘
⊘
⊘
⊘
⊘
⊘
⊘
⊘

REVIEW

DATE COMPLETED: / /

WHAT HAPPENED? (PEOPLE MET, HIGH POINTS, CHALLENGES, EXPECTATIONS VS REALITY)

THE **BEST PART** WAS...

SUCCESS!

PLACE A CHECK HERE TO
TAKE IT OFF YOUR BUCKET LIST

RATE THIS ACTIVITY

☆☆☆☆☆

RETIREMENT IS LIKE A LONG VACATION IN LAS VEGAS: THE GOAL IS TO ENJOY IT THE FULLEST,
BUT NOT SO FULLY THAT YOU RUN OUT OF MONEY. JONATHAN CLEMENTS

ITEM #97:

BUDGET

$

ANTICIPATED DATE

/ /   TO   / /

I WANT TO DO THIS BECAUSE...

ACTION LIST

⊘
⊘
⊘
⊘
⊘
⊘
⊘
⊘
⊘

MAKE IT HAPPEN: HOW? WHEN?

REVIEW

DATE COMPLETED: / /

WHAT HAPPENED? (PEOPLE MET, HIGH POINTS, CHALLENGES, EXPECTATIONS VS REALITY)

SUCCESS! ✓

PLACE A CHECK HERE TO
TAKE IT OFF YOUR BUCKET LIST

RATE THIS ACTIVITY

☆☆☆☆☆

THE **BEST PART** WAS...

MONEY IS SOMETHING YOU GOT TO MAKE IN CASE YOU DON'T DIE. MAX ASNAS

I WANT TO DO THIS BECAUSE...

MAKE IT HAPPEN: HOW? WHEN?

REVIEW

DATE COMPLETED: / /

WHAT HAPPENED? (PEOPLE MET, HIGH POINTS, CHALLENGES, EXPECTATIONS VS REALITY)

THE **BEST PART** WAS...

BUDGET

$

ANTICIPATED DATE

/ /   TO   / /

ACTION LIST

- ⊘
- ⊘
- ⊘
- ⊘
- ⊘
- ⊘
- ⊘
- ⊘
- ⊘

SUCCESS! ✓

PLACE A CHECK HERE TO
TAKE IT OFF YOUR BUCKET LIST

RATE THIS ACTIVITY

☆☆☆☆☆

IT IS TIME I STEPPED ASIDE FOR A LESS EXPERIENCED AND LESS ABLE MAN. SCOTT ELLEDGE

PRIORITY ☆☆☆☆☆　　　　ITEM #99: _____

I WANT TO DO THIS BECAUSE...

_____
_____
_____
_____

MAKE IT HAPPEN: HOW? WHEN?

_____
_____
_____
_____

REVIEW

DATE COMPLETED: ___/___/___

WHAT HAPPENED? (PEOPLE MET, HIGH POINTS, CHALLENGES, EXPECTATIONS VS REALITY)

_____
_____
_____
_____
_____

THE **BEST PART** WAS...

_____
_____
_____
_____
_____

BUDGET

$

ANTICIPATED DATE

/ /　TO　/ /

ACTION LIST

⊘
⊘
⊘
⊘
⊘
⊘
⊘
⊘

SUCCESS! ✓

PLACE A CHECK HERE TO
TAKE IT OFF YOUR BUCKET LIST

RATE THIS ACTIVITY

☆☆☆☆☆

99

ANOTHER GOOD THING ABOUT BEING POOR IS THAT WHEN YOU ARE SEVENTY YOUR CHILDREN WILL NOT HAVE
DECLARED YOU LEGALLY INSANE IN ORDER TO GAIN CONTROL OF YOUR ESTATE. WOODY ALLEN

I WANT TO DO THIS BECAUSE...

MAKE IT HAPPEN: HOW? WHEN?

REVIEW

DATE COMPLETED: / /

WHAT HAPPENED? (PEOPLE MET, HIGH POINTS, CHALLENGES, EXPECTATIONS VS REALITY)

THE **BEST PART** WAS...

BUDGET

$

ANTICIPATED DATE

/ / TO / /

ACTION LIST

⊘
⊘
⊘
⊘
⊘
⊘
⊘
⊘
⊘

SUCCESS! ✓

PLACE A CHECK HERE TO
TAKE IT OFF YOUR BUCKET LIST

RATE THIS ACTIVITY

☆☆☆☆☆

I ADVISE YOU TO GO ON LIVING SOLELY TO ENRAGE THOSE WHO ARE PAYING YOUR ANNUITIES; IT IS THE ONLY PLEASURE I HAVE LEFT. VOLTAIRE

PRIORITY ☆☆☆☆☆   ITEM #101: _____

I WANT TO DO THIS BECAUSE...

_____

_____

_____

_____

MAKE IT HAPPEN: HOW? WHEN?

_____

_____

_____

_____

REVIEW

DATE COMPLETED: / /

_____

WHAT HAPPENED? (PEOPLE MET, HIGH POINTS, CHALLENGES, EXPECTATIONS VS REALITY)

_____

_____

_____

_____

THE **BEST PART** WAS...

_____

_____

_____

_____

_____

BUDGET

$

ANTICIPATED DATE

/ /   TO   / /

ACTION LIST

⊘
⊘
⊘
⊘
⊘
⊘
⊘
⊘
⊘

SUCCESS!

✓

PLACE A CHECK HERE TO
TAKE IT OFF YOUR BUCKET LIST

RATE THIS ACTIVITY

☆☆☆☆☆

Ordering Information
Order more copies of this title at
bit.ly/SuperiorNotebooks

Publisher's Cataloging-in-Publication data
Superior Notebooks.
Retirement Books For Men: Purposeful Retirement Bucket List: Things To Do When You Retire / Superior Notebooks.
p. cm.

ISBN 9781073350537

1. Leisure--Planning. 2. Psychological recreations. 3. Self-actualization (Psychology).--Examinations, questions, etc. I. Superior Notebooks. II. Title.

Made in the USA
Monee, IL
26 June 2023